Novels for Students, Volume 8

Staff

Series Editor: Deborah A. Stanley.

Contributing Editors: Peg Bessette, Sara L. Constantakis, Catherine L. Goldstein, Dwayne D. Hayes, Motoko Fujishiro Huthwaite, Arlene M. Johnson, Angela Yvonne Jones, James E. Person, Jr., Polly Rapp, Erin White.

Editorial Technical Specialist: Tim White.

Managing Editor: Joyce Nakamura.

Research: Victoria B. Cariappa, *Research Team Manager*. Andy Malonis, *Research Specialist*. Tamara C. Nott, Tracie A. Richardson, and Cheryl L. Warnock, *Research Associates*. Jeffrey Daniels, *Research Assistant*.

Permissions: Susan M. Trosky, *Permissions Manager*. Maria L. Franklin, *Permissions Specialist*. Sarah Tomacek, *Permissions Associate*.

Production: Mary Beth Trimper, *Production Director*. Evi Seoud, *Assistant Production Manager*. Cindy Range, *Production Assistant*.

Graphic Services: Randy Bassett, *Image Database Supervisor*. Robert Duncan and Michael Logusz, *Imaging Specialists*. Pamela A. Reed, *Photography Coordinator*. Gary Leach, *Macintosh Artist*.

Product Design: Cynthia Baldwin, *Product Design Manager*. Cover Design: Michelle DiMercurio, *Art Director*. Page Design: Pamela A. E. Galbreath, *Senior Art Director*.

Copyright Notice

Since this page cannot legibly accommodate all copyright notices, the acknowledgments constitute an extension of the copyright notice.

While every effort has been made to secure permission to reprint material and to ensure the reliability of the information presented in this publication, Gale Research neither guarantees the accuracy of the data contained herein nor assumes any responsibility for errors, omissions, or discrepancies. Gale accepts no payment for listing; and inclusion in the publication of any organization, agency, institution, publication, service, or individual does not imply endorsement of the editors or publisher. Errors brought to the attention of the publisher and verified to the satisfaction of the publisher will be corrected in future editions.

This publication is a creative work fully protected by all applicable copyright laws, as well as by misappropriation, trade secret, unfair competition, and other applicable laws. The authors and editors of this work have added value to the underlying factual material herein through one or more of the following: unique and original selection, coordination, expression, arrangement, and classification of the information. All rights to this publication will be vigorously defended.

Copyright © 2000
The Gale Group
27500 Drake Rd.
Farmington Hills, MI 48331-3535

All rights reserved including the right of reproduction in whole or in part in any form.

ISBN 0-7876-3827-7
ISSN 1094-3552

Printed in the United States of America.
10 9 8 7 6 5 4 3 2 1

The Hobbit

J. R. R. Tolkien

1937

Introduction

J. R. R. Tolkien's fantastic novel *The Hobbit; or There and Back Again* was first published in 1937. The enchanting story of tiny, furry-footed Bilbo Baggins and his adventures in Middle-earth ultimately served as the prelude to Tolkien's epic *The Lord of the Rings*, which was published in three volumes during the 1950s. These novels are perhaps the most beloved works of fantasy in the twentieth century.

An eminent Oxford philologist, Tolkien's

translation of ancient myths inspired him to create a world of his own, known as Middle-earth. He spent a great deal of his life developing his own language and mythology for this imaginary realm.

Although the *The Hobbit* garnered favorable reviews on its publication, it wasn't initially a commercial success. However, the novel became extremely popular over the years, eventually selling over one million copies in the United States alone.

Author Biography

Tolkien was born in Bloemfontein, South Africa, on January 3, 1892. His father, Arthur, was an Englishman who had left the Birmingham branch of Lloyds Bank to work for the Bank of Africa. Tolkien and his younger brother were sickly children. Hoping to improve her sons' health, Tolkien's mother, Mabel, took the boys to England in 1895. Arthur remained in Africa to work until his sons sufficiently recovered or he could find a position back in England. Unfortunately, only a few months later, Arthur died of acute peritonitis. Mabel and the boys remained in England.

Tolkien was interested in languages at an early age. His mother began teaching him Latin and Greek when he was seven years old. He also inherited his mother's love for nature and the Catholic church. In 1903 Tolkien won a scholarship to the prestigious King Edward VI School in Birmingham, where his studies included not only the mandatory Latin and Greek, but also Welsh, Old and Middle English, and Old Norse. Tragically, his mother died of diabetes when he was only twelve. A Catholic priest, Father Francis Morgan, cared for the Tolkien brothers after Mabel's death.

At sixteen Tolkien met his future wife, Edith Mary Bratt. Later, his burgeoning love of languages led him to pursue a degree in comparative philology at Exeter College, Oxford University, in 1911. He graduated with honors in 1915, and one year later, he and Bratt married. Shortly after, Tolkien was commissioned a second lieutenant in the English army and left his new bride to fight in World War I. Enclosed in the trenches during the Battle of the Somme, Tolkien contracted a severe case of trench fever and had to be evacuated in 1916.

After returning from the war, Tolkien spent the next several decades building a reputation as a noted scholar and professor at Oxford. He published several esteemed essays, including "Beowulf: The Monsters and the Critics" (1936) and "On Fairy Stories" (1947). Along with C. S. Lewis and Charles Williams, he was an important member of the literary group "The Inklings."

The Hobbit; or There and Back Again was published in 1937 to favorable reviews. It took Tolkien seventeen years before the hobbits returned in *The Lord of the Rings*, a trilogy consisting of *The Fellowship of the Ring* (1954), *The Two Towers* (1954), and *The Return of the Ring* (1955). Although Tolkien's bibliography contains many great works, *The Hobbit* and *The Lord of the Rings* represent the heart of his literary accomplishments. He produced few writings after the success of his 1950s masterpiece. Tolkien died from complications resulting from a bleeding gastric ulcer and a chest infection on September 2, 1973, in Bournemouth, England. However, several of his works were published posthumously, including *The Silmarillion* (1977). Tolkien's work continues to be popular with readers and critics alike.

Plot Summary

The Beginning of the Quest

The Hobbit is set in the imaginary world of Middle-earth. The unidentified narrator begins the tale with a description of hobbits:

> They are (or were) a little people, about half our height, and smaller than the bearded Dwarves. Hobbits have no beards.... They are inclined to be fat in the stomach; they dress in bright colours (chiefly green and yellow); wear no shoes, because their feet grow natural leathery soles and thick warm brown hair like the stuff on their heads (which is curly); have long clever brown fingers, good-natured faces, and laugh deep fruity laughs (especially after dinner, which they have twice a day when they can get it).

The main character, Bilbo Baggins, is a fifty-year-old hobbit living a quiet, comfortable life. This situation is changed by Gandalf, a mysterious wizard, who is looking for someone to go on an adventure with him. Bilbo wants no part of any adventures and quickly excuses himself to go back into his hobbit-hole. Gandalf, secretly amused, scratches a sign into Bilbo's door as it closes.

The next day, Gandalf and a band of thirteen dwarves visit Bilbo. Thorin Oakenshield, the leader of the dwarves, tries to recruit the reluctant hobbit to help recover his father's treasure from the wicked dragon, Smaug. Aided by a map, the group plans to cross the Misty Mountains and the Mirkwood Forest to reach Smaug's hideout. Bilbo is promised a share of the treasure if he will help them. Bilbo eventually concedes.

Along the way, it begins to rain and the group of adventurers lose a large amount of food when one of their ponies, which becomes frightened, jumps into the river. When Bilbo is sent to investigate a light on the side of the road, he finds three trolls sitting by a fire. Bilbo is caught trying to pick one of their pockets, but later escapes into the woods when the trolls begin to argue. The rest of the dwarves are captured as they approach the fire.

Gandalf cleverly uses his magic to cause the trolls to fight amongst themselves. Losing track of time, the trolls turn to stone at dawn. Bilbo and the dwarves search the cave of the trolls, where they discover some food and coins to help them on their journey. Gandalf and Thorin find two jeweled swords, and Bilbo takes a small blade for himself.

After a brief rest, the adventurers continue their journey toward the mountains. Upon reaching the valley of Rivendell, they are greeted by singing elves. They stop at the Last Homely House, where Elrond, chief of the elves, resides. Elrond identifies the blades carried by Gandalf and Thorin; they are magical, powerful goblin-killers. Elrond, also familiar with the runes on Thorin's map, finds a clue regarding an entrance to the Lonely Mountain, where Smaug resides with the treasure. The travelers rest for two weeks before heading into the mountains.

The Misty Mountains

The adventurers are trapped on a narrow pass high in the mountains. As a storm begins, they see stone giants playing with boulders in the pouring rain. Frightened, the dwarves hide in a nearby cave. However, a passage opens in the rear of the cavern, though which goblins enter and abduct them. In the confusion, the dwarves are separated from Gandalf.

Bilbo and the dwarves are brought before the Great Goblin, who is infuriated when he recognizes Thorin's sword. The Great Goblin is ready to execute them. Suddenly, the torches are extinguished, and Gandalf murders the Goblin king. The adventurers flee, fighting off goblins as they escape. They each take turns carrying Bilbo on their backs because he cannot keep up. Bilbo is eventually knocked unconscious.

When Bilbo regains consciousness, he is alone in the cave. Groping through the darkness, he finds a ring on the cavern floor and pockets it. He also discovers that his blade is magical; it glows dimly in the darkness. He wanders to an underground lake, where a slimy, lizard-like creature called Gollum lives. Gollum and Bilbo trade riddles. If Bilbo wins, Gollum agrees to show him the way out. If he loses,

Bilbo becomes Gollum's dinner.

After a series of riddles, Bilbo cleverly stumps Gollum by asking him to guess what he has in his pocket. He does not realize that the ring belongs to Gollum and that it has the power to make its wearer invisible. Gollum cannot guess, and when he goes to fetch his ring, he realizes the answer to Bilbo's riddle. Enraged, he chases Bilbo, but Bilbo slips on the ring, becomes invisible, and sneaks out of the cave.

Bilbo finds Gandalf and the dwarves and surprises them with his sudden appearance. He earns their respect when he tells them the story of his encounter with Gollum and of his escape, but he keeps the secret of the ring to himself. The group travels through a wooded area and, as the sun begins to set, they arrive at a clearing. Frightened by the howls of wolves, they climb up trees to hide.

The Wargs, evil wolves allied with the goblins, appear in the clearing. Gandalf magically lights pine cones on fire and launches them at the Wargs, setting many aflame. However, the goblins appear and build fires at the base of the trees. Meanwhile, the Lord of the Eagles hears the commotion and brings his minions to the rescue. The flock of eagles carries the group to safety.

Gandalf informs his band that he will accompany them to one final destination before they reach the great forest of Mirkwood. He introduces them to Beorn, an enormous shape-shifter of great strength who has the ability to communicate with animals and change into a bear. Beorn provides food for the weary travelers and allows them to rest in his home. He sends them on their way with ponies, food, and water for their journey through the forest, and warns them to keep to the path.

The Forest of Mirkwood

The adventurers leave Gandalf and travel through the forest for several days and nights, slowly exhausting their food and water supply. One night, they see many fires off the path. Hungry, they ignore Beorn's warning and heard for the warm glow of the forest's campfires.

As they approach, everything goes dark. Bilbo falls into an enchanted slumber and giant spiders seize the rest of his comrades. Bilbo recovers and uses his ring to trick the spiders and to release his friends from the webs. A terrific battle ensues and the adventurers escape, only to notice that Thorin is missing.

The next day, the group—except for Bilbo, who wears his ring—is captured by wood elves and brought before their king. The king imprisons the dwarves in his dungeon because they refuse to tell him any information about their mission. Bilbo, discovering that Thorin is also a captive, filches keys from a drunken guard and frees the dwarves. They escape to Long Lake by hiding in barrels used to move goods up and down the river to the town of

Esgaroth.

Smaug and the Battle of Five Armies

The group stops in Esgaroth, a town built in the middle of Long Lake and inhabited by men. Thorin, whose grandfather was once a king allied with the townsmen's ancestors, is greeted warmly. The adventurers are provided food and ponies, and continue their journey by water toward the Lonely Mountain, where Smaug the dragon resides. Once they arrive, they discover a secret opening. Bilbo sneaks into the dragon's lair, steals a cup, and brings it back to the dwarves to prove his worth as a burglar.

The disturbed dragon leaves his lair to find the thief. Bilbo and the dwarves take cover, but they are unable to save their pack animals. Smaug devours the ponies and returns to his lair. Bilbo agrees to sneak back into Smaug's lair for further investigation. Bilbo, now invisible, intrigues the dragon with flattery and riddles. He discovers that Smaug has a weak point in his breast. After Bilbo flees the lair, Smaug leaves and attacks the town of Esgaroth. The adventurers enter the unguarded cave and locate the stolen treasure. Bilbo finds the Arkenstone of Thrain, the great jewel of the dwarves.

Meanwhile, Smaug sets Esgaroth on fire. Bard, a human, finds Smaug's weak point and shoots an arrow into the dragon's heart, killing him. Upon learning of the dragon's death, the King of the Wood Elves and his army join the humans and together they set off for the Lonely Mountain to claim the treasure.

A raven informs Thorin that Smaug is dead and that the humans and the elves are coming for the treasure. The dwarves fortify the only open entrance to the mountain. Thorin sends the raven to fetch his cousin's army. The men and elves arrive and demand a share of the treasure; Thorin refuses. The men and elves decide to camp around the mountain, but Bilbo sneaks out with the Arkenstone.

Hoping to avoid bloodshed, Bilbo gives Bard and the King of the Wood Elves the Arkenstone to use in bargaining with Thorin. They offer Bilbo sanctuary, but he is loyal to the dwarves and determined to rejoin them. On his way back, he is heartened to discover that Gandalf has returned and is camping with the men.

The next morning, the humans and elves show the Arkenstone to Thorin. When Bilbo admits that he gave the jewel to the men, Thorin accuses Bilbo of treachery and threatens to throw him off the mountain. Thorin releases Bilbo, but still refuses to share the treasure. Thorin's cousin Dain arrives.

An army of goblins and Wargs descends upon both warring groups, however, and the two sides are compelled to join forces. Even Thorin overcomes his greed and bravely joins the fight. A fierce battle ensues, and the goblins appear to have the upper hand. However, Bilbo's spirits are lifted when he sees the Lord of the Eagles arriving with a huge flock. Bilbo is once again knocked unconscious when a rock hits his head.

The End of the Tale

Bilbo awakens to a deathly quiet until he hears a man calling for him. Bilbo removes his ring and is brought to a tent where Thorin lays dying. Thorin apologizes for treating Bilbo badly and commends the hobbit's wisdom and bravery. Bilbo weeps when Thorin dies; he also discovers that Beorn arrived after the eagles to help turn the tide of the battle. The hobbit accepts a share of the treasure and leaves with Gandalf and Beorn, heading for home.

The story ends with a short epilogue a few years later when Gandalf and the dwarf, Balin, visit Bilbo. Bilbo learns that the dwarves are content and prosperous, and that Bard has led many of the men of Esgaroth to rebuild Dale, a city destroyed by Smaug.

Characters

Bilbo Baggins

A short, peaceful hobbit, Bilbo Baggins is the protagonist of the novel. He considers himself a typical hobbit; that is, until Gandalf and the dwarves appear at his door. Although he initially hesitates, Bilbo joins the adventure to find the stolen treasure.

As the story progresses, Bilbo proves himself to be a clever burglar and resourceful companion. He proves his courage when he cuts the dwarves from the webs in Mirkwood and battles the spiders. He later frees the dwarves from the prison of the wood elves. His keen observation of Smaug ultimately reveals the dragon's weak point. One of his most valiant acts is giving the Arkenstone, Thorin's beloved jewel, to the men and elves in a bold attempt to avoid bloodshed. Out of loyalty he returns to the dwarves even though he knows he risks Thorin's wrath.

Balin

Balin is one of the band of thirteen dwarves led by Thorin. Years later he visits Bilbo.

Bard

A courageous human, Bard slays the dragon.

Afterward, he goes to the mountain to claim the treasure. He attempts to bargain fairly with Thorin, but the dwarf is blinded by greed. A war over the treasure is avoided only when the goblins attack. After the forces of good defeat the goblins, Bard rebuilds Dale and the city becomes prosperous under his leadership.

Beorn

Beorn is a shape-shifter. A peaceful creature, he allows the band of adventurers to stay in his cabin. He helps turn the tide of the Battle of Five Armies when he appears and kills the goblin general. He also protects Gandalf and Bilbo on part of their journey home.

Bifur

Bifur is one of the band of thirteen dwarves led by Thorin.

Bofur

Bofur is one of the band of thirteen dwarves led by Thorin.

Bombur

Bombur is one of Thorin's band of dwarves. He slips into the enchanted river in Mirkwood Forest and falls into a magical sleep, forcing the party to carry him along.

Dain

Dain is Thorin's cousin from the Iron Hills. Thorin sends a raven to summon Dain and his army to help defend the treasure under the Lonely Mountain from the men and elves after Smaug is slain, and Dain joins forces with the men to defeat the evil creatures. He is crowned King under the Mountain after Thorin dies in the Battle of Five Armies.

Dori

Dori is one of the band of thirteen dwarves led by Thorin.

Dwalin

Dwalin is a member of Thorin's band of dwarves.

Elrond

Elrond is the master of the Last Homely House of Rivendell. He gives Bilbo, Gandalf, and the dwarves sanctuary. A mix of elf and human, he is the peace-loving chieftain of all the elves in the valley. He identifies the swords carried by Gandalf and Thorin, and he is able to read the runes on Thorin's map.

Fili

Fili and his brother Kili are the youngest of the dwarves. He perishes defending Thorin during the Battle of Five Armies.

Gandalf

A mighty wizard, Gandalf convinces the dwarves to recruit Bilbo Baggins for the adventure to reclaim the treasure. Ageless and wise, he alone recognizes the potential greatness in Bilbo. Gandalf is also brave, as evidenced by his decapitation of the Great Goblin. He tends to appear at the most opportune moments and is familiar with all aspects of Middle-earth.

Gloin

Gloin is one of the band of thirteen dwarves led by Thorin.

Goblins

Goblins are evil creatures. After Gandalf slays the Great Goblin with a magical sword, the elves hunt down the adventurers. The goblin army almost defeats the forces of good in the Battle of Five Armies, but the Lord of the Eagles and Beorn turn the tide of the conflict. At the end of the story, most of the goblins in the region have been annihilated.

Gollum

Gollum is a slimy, lizard-like creature living

on a rock in the middle of a cold lake underneath the Misty Mountains. He possesses the powerful ring of invisibility. (How it came into his possession is revealed in *Lord of the Rings*). Bilbo accidentally discovers the ring and wins a war of riddles with Gollum. It is only when Gollum attacks Bilbo in a rage that the hobbit actually discovers the power of the ring. Bilbo leaves Gollum, pathetic and weeping over the loss of "his precious" ring, in the tunnels below the Misty Mountains.

Kili

Kili and his brother Fili, Thorin's nephews, are the youngest of the dwarves. He is killed defending his uncle during the Battle of Five Armies.

King of the Wood Elves

The King of the Wood Elves captures Thorin and the rest of the dwarves when they leave the beaten path in the forest of Mirkwood. He demands to know the purpose of their journey. Bilbo frees the dwarves before he can find out, but the King soon learns of their intentions after Smaug's demise. He gathers an army of elves to earn a piece of the treasure. He recognizes Bilbo's wisdom when the hobbit offers the Arkenstone.

Media Adaptations

- *The Hobbit* was adapted into an animated film for television by Jules Bass and Arthur Rankin in 1978. The film features the voices of Orson Bean as Bilbo, John Huston as Gandalf, and Richard Boone as Smaug. It is available on videotape.
- There are several audiotape versions of *The Hobbit*, including a 1992 BBC adaptation from Bantam Doubleday.

Lord of the Eagles

The Lord of the Eagles leads his flock to save Bilbo, Gandalf, and the dwarves when they are trapped in the trees by goblins and Wargs. Later, they join the humans, elves, and dwarves in the Battle of Five Armies to defeat the goblins. Dain rewards their efforts with golden collars.

Nori

Nori is one of the band of thirteen dwarves led by Thorin.

Thorin Oakenshield

Thorin is the brave leader of a band of thirteen dwarves. His grandfather was the King under the Mountain until Smaug drove the dwarves away and destroyed the human city of Dale. At the start of the novel he seeks to reclaim the treasure of his ancestors and take his throne. When Smaug is finally defeated, Thorin's greed for the treasure, especially his lust for the Arkenstone, almost leads to a disastrous war with the humans and elves. He even banishes Bilbo from his camp when the hobbit gives away the Arkenstone. Thorin is redeemed when the goblins and Wargs attack in the Battle of Five Armies. He joins the humans and elves to fight the wicked creatures and dies from his wounds.

Oin

Oin is one of the band of thirteen dwarves led by Thorin.

Ori

Ori is one of the band of thirteen dwarves led by Thorin.

Smaug

Smaug is a wicked, fire-breathing dragon. He is extremely powerful, intelligent, and cruel. Years before, he destroyed the peaceful, wealthy community of dwarves under the Lonely Mountain and the human city of Dale. The dwarves and humans were trading partners and enjoyed a friendly relationship. The human survivors built Esgaroth, a town in the middle of the Long Lake.

When Bilbo and the dwarves arrive at the Lonely Mountain, Smaug has been in hibernation for quite some time. Wearing the ring of invisibility, Bilbo awakens the evil monster; fortunately, he is clever enough to find Smaug's vulnerabilities. Later Smaug attacks Esgaroth and Bard kills the dragon.

Spiders

Giant, intelligent spiders lurk in the forest of Mirkwood. Bilbo frees the dwarves from webs when he distracts the spiders; once free, the group slaughters the spiders.

Trolls

The trolls are described as large, nasty, and

strong. At one point, they capture the dwarves and plan to eat them. Gandalf saves the day by spreading dissension amongst the trolls; as a result, they argue until dawn and turn to stone.

Wargs

The Wargs are evil wolves. They take part in the Battle of Five Armies.

Themes

Good vs. Evil

The conflict between good and evil is the main theme of Tolkien's *Hobbit*. The good creatures strive for a peaceful existence, while the evil creatures cause suffering. In the novel, the quest to reclaim the treasure is considered a righteous cause. Even Bilbo, a gentle hobbit reluctant to get involved, is ultimately convinced to join the quest because he believes it to be a noble mission.

The wizard Gandalf also believes in a good cause. He is a wise and just being who wanders the realm improving the quality of life. A decent judge of character, he recognizes Bilbo's resourcefulness. Elrond, Beorn, and Bard are also examples of the many good and courageous beings who live in Middle-earth.

Evil creatures constantly threaten the forces of good. The mighty dragon Smaug destroys towns and kills their inhabitants. The goblins and Wargs are sneaky, cruel, and vicious. Horrible, enormous spiders lurk in the forests of Mirkwood, preying upon those who venture away from the main path.

There are shades of gray, as in real life. Good characters also can do bad things. For example, although most would consider stealing immoral, Bilbo is recruited as a thief. Thorin, a brave and honorable dwarf, is temporarily blinded by greed and he almost causes a war over the treasure before he redeems himself in the Battle of Five Armies. In any case, the conflict between good and evil is a major theme in the novel. Ultimately the virtuous are triumphant.

Fate and Chance

The roles of fate and chance are addressed in *The Hobbit*. While many of the events in the novel seem to occur by chance, especially Bilbo's discovery of the ring of power that grants him invisibility, the characters ostensibly are ruled by fate. For example, at the end of the book, Bilbo refers to the "prophecies of old songs" that turn out to be true. Gandalf replies:

> Surely you don't disbelieve the prophecies, because you had a hand in bringing them about yourself? You don't really suppose, do you, that all your adventures and escapes were managed by mere luck, just for your sole benefit?

In this passage Gandalf implies that fate partly determined the course of Bilbo's adventures.

While Tolkien did not ignore the importance of free will and chance in *The Hobbit*, he also recognized prophecy and fate as core elements of mythology. Thus, as a modern myth-maker, he worked these themes into the framework of his fantasies.

Friendship

In the novel, friendship often results from peculiar alliances. At first, Bilbo and the dwarves do not trust each other: Bilbo finds the dwarves rude and coarse; the dwarves believe that Bilbo is timid and meek. Yet Bilbo eventually gains their respect with his cleverness, courage, and wisdom. He learns that the dwarves, however brusque and ill-mannered they may be, are loyal and brave friends. At the end of the novel Bilbo is officially made an "elf-friend."

Gandalf befriends any creature on the side of good, particularly hobbits, dwarves, and elves. He recruits Beorn, the mighty shape-shifter, as a valuable ally.

Even evil creatures have friends, as exemplified by the alliance between the goblins and Wargs.

Death

In *J. R. R. Tolkien: Architect of Middle-earth*, Daniel Grotta quotes Tolkien, who once stated that the principle theme of his work was death:

> If you really come down to any really large story that interests people and holds their attention for a considerable time, it is practically always a human story, and it is practically [always] about one thing all the time: *death*. The inevitability of death.

Although Tolkien was referring to his epic novel *The Lord of the Rings*, death is also an important theme in *The Hobbit*. The good characters in this novel risk death at almost every turn. They encounter incredibly vicious creatures such as trolls, goblins, wolves, spiders, and a fire-breathing dragon. They almost end up as meals for the giant spiders and trolls.

They also face such natural hazards as storms, treacherous mountain passes, and the seemingly endless forest of Mirkwood. They are often in danger of starvation. Fortunately, they have powerful allies like Gandalf and Beorn on their side. In addition, the adventurers also have magical items to aid them: the swords they take from the trolls and Bilbo's ring of power.

It is not until the end of the story that death claims any of the major characters. Thorin's nephews, Fili and Kili, are killed during the Battle of Five Armies. Thorin is mortally wounded during this battle.

War

War plays an important part in the climax of *The Hobbit*. When Thorin fortifies the Lonely Mountain after the death of Smaug, a war between the forces of good appears imminent. The men and elves are in a stalemate with Thorin's band over the treasure.

Topics for Further Study

- Tolkien composed songs and verses for the creatures of Middle-earth to sing. Choose an event from the novel, such as the Battle of Five Armies or Bilbo's fight with the spiders, and write a verse based on the event. Add music, prerecorded or original.

- Do some research into Norse or Greek mythology. What elements do the various myths share with the Middle-earth of *The Hobbit?*

- Explain what happens between Bard and the Master of Esgaroth after Smaug's death. Are there examples in contemporary world politics that reflect the dynamics of this situation?

- Using computer graphics, painting, sculpture, or another type of artistic media, create a character or scene from *The Hobbit*.

However, armies of goblins and Wargs attack the humans, elves, and dwarves camped at the mountain. Thorin overcomes his greed and the forces of good unite to fight evil in the Battle of the Five Armies. Although the losses are great, the forces of good are victorious with the help of Beorn and the Lord of the Eagles.

The end of the war signals the close of the novel. Most of the goblins and Wargs have been driven away. Thorin dies, and Dain is made King under the Mountain in Thorin's place. The treasure is divided to everyone's satisfaction. Bard rebuilds the city of Dale, and both Dale and Esgaroth prosper. Finally, Bilbo returns to the peace and quiet of his hobbit-hole.

Style

Fantasy and Mythology

The Hobbit is considered a masterpiece of fantasy. There is often a tendency among scholars of literature to deride genres such as fantasy and science fiction; however, Tolkien's books are so imaginative and brilliantly conceived that he has earned a great deal of critical respect.

Tolkien's imaginary world was derived from mythology. He believed that myth was a tool that cultures use to build bridges of understanding between generations.

Although Tolkien invented hobbits, most of the creatures that populate Middle-earth were borrowed from the myths of other cultures. Beings akin to *The Hobbit*'s dwarves, elves, and trolls, as well as Smaug the dragon, can be found in many ancient legends and myths. In addition, magic and magical objects are incorporated within the plot of the story, as in so many other fantastic tales. The quest motif advances the narrative, as it does in Arthurian legend. Virtue, embodied in the heroism and humility of the characters, is ultimately triumphant as it is in most classic mythology.

Narration

The story is told in the third person, mostly

from Bilbo's point of view. However, the narrator acts as a storyteller familiar with the history, geography, language, and demographics of Middle-earth. The telling is informal, as if it were a campfire or bedtime story.

The narrator also knows how the story is going to end and functions as a link between Middle-earth and the present.

Setting

The Hobbit is set in the enchanted realm of Middle-earth, which has a topography much like that of Earth, with forests, rivers, mountains, *etc.* Tolkien wanted the world of the novel to be somewhat familiar to readers. Thus, he drew from his childhood experiences—particularly those of his hometown of Sarehole, which inspired the Shire of the hobbits—to construct some of the geographies of Middle-earth. His memories of a climbing expedition in the Swiss Alps during his youth inspired the Misty Mountains.

Humor

Although much of *The Hobbit* is dark, humor is often used to break up the tension. Bilbo's meek and fussy behavior in the beginning of the novel is one example. The dwarves, as they clean up the mess they have made in Bilbo's hobbit-hole, sing a song about breaking plates, because "That's what Bilbo Baggins hates…."

There is humor in even the most dangerous situations. The scenes when Bilbo is threatened by Gollum, or when he flatters Smaug, are good examples.

Historical Context

Pre-World War II England

When *The Hobbit* was published in 1937, Europe was in turmoil. The German dictator Adolf Hitler made no secret of his plan to expand German territory and rid his country of certain minorities, in particular the Jewish people. Many English politicians, including Winston Churchill, recognized the potential danger of Hitler's regime. However, British Prime Minister Neville Chamberlain sought to avoid conflict with Hitler. In March 1938, Hitler's forces annexed Austria and created a crisis throughout Europe.

Chamberlain's controversial response was a policy of "appeasement," which allowed Hitler certain territories like Austria. He signed the Munich Pact with Hitler after the Austrian annexation to avoid war and proclaimed, "I believe it is peace in our time." A month later, Germany occupied the Czech Sudetenland. Yet when Germany invaded Poland on September 1, 1939, Great Britain and France declared war on Germany two days later. Chamberlain was forced to resign in May, 1940; Churchill took over and led the country through the difficult years of World War II.

With the start of World War II, constant air raids and threats of invasion from the European continent endangered the English. Meanwhile,

English casualties mounted and the German forces (as well as Benito Mussolini's Italian army) gained much ground early in the war. Tolkien believed that fantasy literature comforted people in such anxious and difficult times, and certainly *The Hobbit* serves as an excellent example of escapist literature.

Oxford University and the Inklings

Oxford University is the oldest English-speaking university in the world. Since 1096 teaching has existed at Oxford in some form. The university is comprised of thirty-nine independent, self-governing colleges, including Exeter College, which Tolkien entered in 1911.

At Oxford, Tolkien studied the classics, including Greek and Roman languages, literature, art, history, and philosophy, as well as modern languages, literature, and philosophy. He was awarded a degree with first-class honors in English Language and Literature just before he left for France to fight in World War I.

After the war Tolkien returned to Oxford to work as a teacher and tutor for the English School. Over the next several years, he established a reputation as a brilliant philologist and linguist. From the mid-1930s until 1962, Tolkien was part of an informal literary club at Oxford known as the Inklings. The group included several famous English writers, poets, essayists, and critics of the time, including Tolkien's close friend C. S. Lewis, as well as Owen Barfield, Hugo Dyson, and Charles

Williams.

Compare & Contrast

- **Late 1930s:** Hitler occupies Austria and the Czech Sudetenland in 1938. British Prime Minister Neville Chamberlain adopts his controversial "appeasement" policy in an effort to mollify Hitler. The strategy is doomed when Hitler's aggression leads Germany to invade Poland on September 1, 1939. Two days later Great Britain and France declare war on Germany.

  Today: The European Economic Community (EEC) is an economic powerhouse. A new European currency, the Euro, is issued. However, political events threaten economic progress for Europe as the conflict in Yugoslavia wreaks havoc in the Balkans. Also, Serbian aggression in Kosovo leads to the NATO bombing of Belgrade.

- **Late 1930s:** In South Africa, Tolkien's birth place, the Native Laws Amendment Act is passed. This law extends the long-established system of pass laws, which require blacks to carry special papers to stay in the cities. This law is only one in a series over many years establishing the apartheid (apartness) system in South Africa.

Today: Nelson Mandela retires as President of South Africa. Imprisoned in 1961 for protesting the apartheid system, he was freed in 1988 and elected president of South Africa. Apartheid has been dismantled for many years, yet the effects of the policy are still evident throughout South African society.

- **Late 1930s:** With the advent of World War II, military production provides a spark for American manufacturing and industrial production. As a result, the United States begins to reverse the economic collapse of the Great Depression.

  Today: The economies of the United States and Europe are strong. Due to the government's efforts to adopt a more democratic system, the Russian economy experiences a difficult transition. Japan suffers from a recession because of various factors, including a banking crisis.

The Inklings would read and discuss their writings with each other. Many of the members encouraged Tolkien to publish *The Hobbit*. Tolkien also read most of *The Lord of the Rings* to the group years before it was published. The Inklings dissolved when Lewis became ill in 1962 and died the following year.

Critical Overview

Perhaps the most important critique of *The Hobbit* came from ten-year-old Raynor Unwin, the son of English publisher Sir Stanley Unwin. According to Daniel Grotta, in his biography *J. R. R. Tolkien: Architect of Middle-earth*, young Unwin earned between a shilling and a half-crown for reviewing children's literature. His assessment of *The Hobbit* is as follows:

> Bilbo Baggins was a hobbit who lived in his hobbit hole and *never* went for adventures, at last Gandalf the wizard and his dwarves persuaded him to go. He had a very exciting time fighting goblins and Wargs. At last they got to the lonely mountain: Smaug, the dragon who guards it, is killed and after a terrific battle with the goblins he returned home—rich!

This book, with the help of maps, does not need any illustrations. It is good and should appeal to all children between the ages of 5 and 9.

Raynor Unwin said years later, "I wouldn't say my report was the best critique of *The Hobbit* that has been written, but it was good enough to ensure that it was published."

The Hobbit was published in 1937, and most

reviewers concurred with Unwin's positive assessment. Although the book was primarily viewed as children's literature, several reviewers emphasized the book's appeal to older readers. A reviewer (believed to be C. S. Lewis) in the London *Times Literary Supplement* wrote, "It must be understood that this is a children's book only in the sense that the first of many readings can be undertaken in the nursery."

In the *New York Times*, Anne T. Eaton asserted, "Boys and girls from 8 years on have already given *The Hobbit* an enthusiastic welcome, but this is a book with no age limits." Because Tolkien believed that mythology and fairy tales helped bridge the gap between generations, he would have been pleased with these assessments.

Despite the excellent reviews, *The Hobbit* was not initially a financial success for Tolkien. However, the commercial success of *The Lord of the Rings* trilogy during the 1950s also affected the sales of its predecessor. Tolkien lived to see *The Hobbit* sell over a million copies in the United States alone. It continues to be one of the best-selling fantasy titles in print.

Tolkien's work has generated a great deal of scholarly criticism, primarily concentrating on *The Lord of the Rings*. Much commentary focuses on the creation, history, and languages of Middle-earth. Several authors, including Edmund Fuller, have looked for allegory (characters or events used to represent things or abstract ideas to convey a message or teach a lesson) in Tolkien's work.

However, the author vehemently denied the use of allegory in his books. In his introduction to the Ballantine edition of *The Lord of the Rings*, he wrote:

> I cordially dislike allegory in all its manifestations, and always have done so since I grew old and wary enough to detect its presence. I much prefer history, true or feigned, with its varied applicability to the reader. I think that many confuse applicability with allegory; but the one resides in the freedom of the reader, and the other in the purported domination of the author.

The Hobbit is first and foremost a grand adventure, a tale of good overcoming evil.

What Do I Read Next?

- Tolkien's epic *The Lord of the Rings* is essential reading for those interested in Middle-earth. The novel contains three volumes: *The Fellowship of the Ring* (1954), *The Two Towers* (1955), and *The Return of the King* (1955). It chronicles the adventures of Frodo, Bilbo's nephew, and his quest to destroy the ring of power discovered in *The Hobbit*.

- *The Silmarillion* (1977) was published after Tolkien's death. His son, Christopher, compiled the book from various fragments written before *The Hobbit* and *The Lord of the Rings*. It details the ancient history of Middle-earth.

- C. S. Lewis wrote a seven-volume children's fantasy series called *The Chronicles of Narnia*. The series follows the adventures of four children who discover a magical world of talking animals, witches, and dwarves behind a wardrobe in an old house. The first book published in the series, *The Lion, the Witch, and the Wardrobe* (1950), is a good place to start.

- Daniel Grotta's *J. R. R. Tolkien: Architect of Middle-earth* (1976) is a compelling account of Tolkien's life and works. Grotta discusses the influences on Tolkien's fiction and provides an in-depth analysis of his major works.

- Fritz Leiber wrote dozens of stories featuring his Fafhrd, a barbarian, and the Gray Mouser, a cynical thief. Their adventures in the world of Newhon are exciting and original. *Ill Met in Lankhmar* (1995) contains the first two collections of his Fafhrd and Gray Mouser stories. It is a good introduction to the fascinating realm of Newhon.

- Author Michael Moorcock's *Elric* series is captivating for those readers interested in fantasy literature. The protagonist, Elric, is an evil elf whose sword, Stormbringer, steals souls. *Elric of Melnibone* (1972) is the first novel in the series.

Sources

Peter Beagle, in an introduction to *The Hobbit*, by J. R. R. Tolkien, Houghton Mifflin, 1973.

Anne Eaton, in the *New York Times*, March 13, 1938, p. 12.

Daniel Grotta, in *J. R. R. Tolkien: Architect of Middle-earth*, Running Press, 1976, pp. 85-105.

Times Literary Supplement, October 2, 1937, p. 714.

For Further Study

David Day, in *A Tolkien Bestiary*, Random House, 1998, 286 p.

> Surveys the beasts, deities, and other creatures that exist in Middle-earth.

Karen Wynn Fonstad, in *The Atlas of Middle-earth*, Houghton Mifflin, 1991, 210 p.

> Detailed maps of Middle-earth, including war and other thematic maps.

Robert Foster, in *A Guide to Middle-earth*, Ballantine Books, 1974, 291 p.

> A directory to all the proper names appearing in *The Hobbit, The Lord of the Rings, The Adventures of Tom Bombadil*, and *The Road Goes Ever On*.

Neil D. Isaacs and Rose A. Zimbardo, in *Tolkien and the Critics*, University of Notre Dame Press, 1968, 296 p.

> A collection of essays analyzing Tolkien's *The Lord of the Rings*, including contributions from C. S. Lewis and W. H. Auden.

Paul H. Kocher, in *Master of Middle-earth: The Fiction of J. R. R. Tolkien*, Houghton Mifflin Co., 1973, 247 p.

> A comprehensive study of Tolkien's major works.

J. R. R. Tolkien, in *The Tolkien Reader*, Ballantine Books, Inc., 1974, 200 p.

> Contains some of Tolkien's lesser-known fiction and poetry.

Lightning Source UK Ltd.
Milton Keynes UK
UKHW020634220822
407644UK00009B/1092

9 781375 391610